M IS FOR MINDFULNESS

AN ALPHABET BOOK OF CALM

Illustrated by

CAROlyn SU

A

AWARENESS

Noticing what's going on in your mind and body, right now

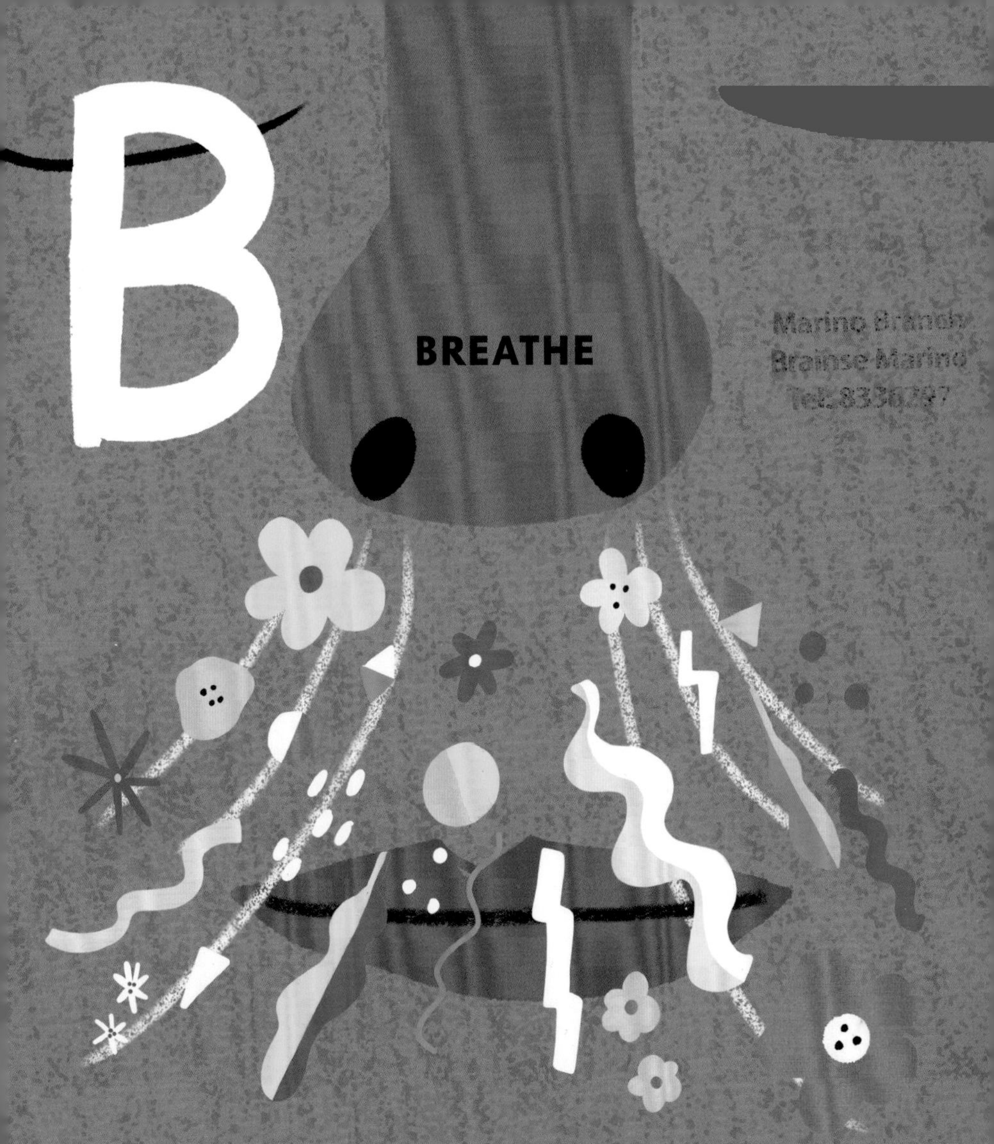

B

BREATHE

**When you fill your lungs
with air and then let it go**

CURIOSITY

Being interested in the world and open to learning more

D

DISTRACTION

Things that make it difficult to pay attention to what you're doing

E

EMOTION

Your feelings, such as happiness or sadness, which come and go

F

FOCUS

Aiming your mind at just one thing

SPRINKL

**Keeping your heart soft,
like a feather**

H
HOPE
The feeling you get that
things will be OK in the end

INTUITION

Understanding the world through your feelings

JOY

A feeling of intense happiness

K

KIND

Being good to yourself and to others

LISTEN

When you take in the sounds around you

MINDFULNESS

Paying attention to your thoughts, feelings and senses in this moment

N

NOW

DFULNESS
Paying attention to
your thoughts, feelings
and senses in this moment
NOW
The present time, as you read this book

The present time, as you read this book

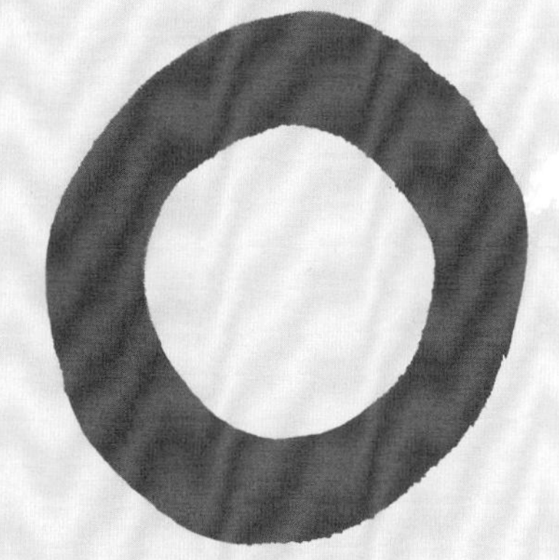

OPEN

When your mind is as free and as wide as the sky

P

PEACE

Feeling calm inside

Q
QUIET
When there’s no noise or busyness or trouble

RELAX

Staying still and letting yourself go loose and floppy

SENSATION

A feeling in your body – how does your body feel right now?

THOUGHTS

What passes through your mind as images or words

**When you feel sad or bad –
these feelings pass with time**

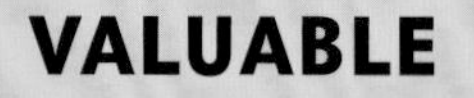

VALUABLE

When something is important, like you are

WONDER

To imagine each and every possibility

X
EXERCISE
Moving your body to help you focus on the present

YOU

The amazing person that you are

Z

ZIP

When you zip your lips closed and just listen to your thoughts